COLOSSIANS & PHILEMON

Meet Me in the Bible Studies

Colossians and Philemon

The Story of Abraham

"Simple and straightforward, Meet Me in the Bible is a wonderful resource to gain foundational skills in studying the Bible. If you want to feel confident in mining Scripture for God's truths and applying it to your life, this is an incredible guide."

Laura Wifler, Cofounder, Risen Motherhood; coauthor, *Risen Motherhood: Gospel Hope for Everyday Moments*

"I was greeted by the bright smile of Colleen Searcy over thirty years ago when I walked into a youth group in West Texas as a freckle-faced, curly headed, unbelieving teenager. Over the last three decades, I have watched Colleen cling to God's word, teach God's word, sing God's word, and live God's word. If you are looking to *meet* God in the Scriptures, I can think of no better guide than my friend Colleen. She will help you taste and see that the Lord is good!"

Shane Barnard, singer-songwriter, Shane and Shane

"Colleen Searcy is one of my favorite Bible teachers. You will sense her open-armed ministry within the framework of her Meet Me in the Bible series, in which she's thoughtfully prepared a table for women to feast on God's word. Whether you are an individual hungry to know God more, a small group desiring an accessible way to study together, or a women's ministry leader looking for a foundational resource for your teaching team, the Meet Me in the Bible series is a trustworthy guide."

Caroline Saunders, author, *Come Home: Tracing God's Promise of Home through Scripture*

"I've benefited from Colleen's wisdom, teaching, and partnership in ministry for a number of years. She is a gifted Bible teacher who uses her skills to invite others into biblical literacy. In the Meet Me in the Bible series, she provides what few studies do—an opportunity for women to gather for both in-person teaching and discussion. You will be equipped to not only study for yourself but also cultivate teaching gifts in the lives of the women in your church. I can't wait to recommend this to my ministry friends."

Courtney Reissig, author, *Teach Me to Feel: Worshiping through the Psalms in Every Season of Life*

"As the CEO of a worldwide mission agency, I highly recommend Colleen Searcy's Meet Me in the Bible series for anyone interested in going deeper in their study of the Bible. Colleen uses a structured approach with guiding prompts that are fully interactive and enhance your reflection on Scripture. These books are helpful resources for pursuing individual study or leading a Bible study group, and these studies are culturally relevant for all groups of people. Meet Me in the Bible is an excellent and well-rounded framework that can make studying the Bible a more engaging and enriching experience for anyone."

Kurt Nelson, CEO, East-West Ministries

"I have seen firsthand the fruit of Meet Me in the Bible. Colleen's accessible framework for studying the Scripture has had a large and lasting impact on our church. Many in our congregation are still reaping the benefits of her investment in our women's ministry. If you are a seasoned student of the Scripture or are just getting started, Meet Me in the Bible will launch you into a greater exploration of the Bible and a deeper enjoyment of the God it reveals."

JR Vassar, Lead Pastor, Church at the Cross, Grapevine, Texas; author, *Glory Hunger*

MEET ME IN THE BIBLE

COLOSSIANS & PHILEMON

AN 8-WEEK BIBLE STUDY

COLLEEN D. SEARCY

Foreword by Jen Wilkin

WHEATON, ILLINOIS

Colossians and Philemon: An 8-Week Bible Study

Published by Crossway
1300 Crescent Street
Wheaton, Illinois 60187

Tool 1, "Bible Timeline," designed by Brooke Hawkins.

Definitions in Tool 4, "The Attributes of God," are taken from or informed by *The ABCs of God* by Jill Nelson. © 1998, 2016 Jill Nelson. Illustrations Truth78.org. All rights reserved. Used by permission.

Cover illustration and design by Brooke Hawkins

First printing 2025

Printed in China

Trade paperback ISBN: 978-1-4335-9687-2
ePub ISBN: 978-1-4335-9689-6
PDF ISBN: 978-1-4335-9688-9

Crossway is a publishing ministry of Good News Publishers.

RRD 34 33 32 31 30 29 28 27 26 25
15 14 13 12 11 10 9 8 7 6 5 4 3 2

CONTENTS

FOREWORD

For the past twenty-five years, my primary place of ministry has been the local church, and my primary aim has been to build Bible literacy among women. So, naturally, any time I'm asked to endorse a resource, I ask myself how it will serve that context. That's why I'm particularly excited to bring to your attention the Meet Me in the Bible series.

When evaluating a resource, I hold two important questions in view: (1) Is this from a trustworthy voice? and (2) Does this challenge those who use it to grow in their ability to read and understand the Scriptures? I want to help answer both of those questions for you as you consider how the Meet Me in the Bible series might help you personally, or those you serve in your church.

In terms of the trustworthiness of the author, I can speak with confidence that Colleen Searcy is an excellent guide. I first met Colleen in 2008, about a year after moving to Dallas and joining a new church. I was looking for other women in the church who shared my desire to see women equipped with solid discipleship opportunities. Colleen and I went to coffee, and I knew I had found a like-minded partner. Since that time, we have together taught, written curriculum, led teams, and prayed—all from that desire to see God's daughters grounded in the Scriptures. Colleen is not only theologically and biblically solid; she is a gifted teacher, humble and kind, and a faithful friend.

In terms of the usefulness of the resource, Meet Me in the Bible so closely aligns with my own philosophy of teaching that I can recommend it eagerly. It's a brilliant combination of a Scripture journal and a guide for growing in Bible literacy. It encourages the user to practice the time-tested method of "observe, interpret, apply" in a way that allows understanding to grow gradually. It presses us to be active learners rather than passive consumers, not rushing to commentaries, but sitting with the text, patiently waiting for our own understanding to begin to emerge. For those who know my method and Bible studies, Meet Me in the Bible will feel familiar in the best ways.

It is a streamlined approach suitable for personal study as well as an excellent foundation for group discussion and teaching environments.

The skills taught in each Meet Me in the Bible study will help you understand a particular book of the Bible better. But they will also help you understand *any* book of the Bible better as you grow in your ability to use those skills. And because application focuses on relationship—with God, self, and others—these skills will help you to live and love like a Christ follower.

So it is my pleasure to commend to you both a trusted guide and a trustworthy resource. My guess is that if you had come to coffee with Colleen and me on that day some years ago, you would have shared our excitement to see women growing in their love of the Scriptures and of the God they proclaim. What we want for you is to be able to serve your local church, whether in a classroom or a living room, with good tools and the confidence to use them. My prayer is that you would take what Colleen has created and combine it with an invitation to the women God has placed in your sphere of influence—a simple invitation: Meet me in the Bible! No sweeter fellowship is found than in that meeting place. May your time spent there yield the richest of treasures.

JEN WILKIN
Bible teacher; author, *Women of the Word*; *None Like Him*; and *In His Image*

MEET ME IN THE BIBLE

A Simple Framework for Reading the Bible and Enjoying God

God delights in revealing himself, and one of the primary ways he reveals himself is through the Bible. My deep desire is for people to know and enjoy God through the study of his word. I want people with all kinds of personalities and learning styles to grow in confidence that they can read and study their Bibles. This framework of Bible study was designed to provide helpful structure and a lot of freedom for the studier.

The *Why* behind Meet Me in the Bible

Meet Me in the Bible is a simple, five-step framework designed to help you read your Bible. It is not a fill-in-the-blank study. After numerous conversations with women over many years of ministry, I've found that countless women do Bible studies, yet few feel confident opening the Bible and reading it on their own. And although many women desire to lead a Bible study, few feel equipped to do so. Meet Me in the Bible offers a method to help you do both.

How to Use Meet Me in the Bible

This framework was designed for either individual or group Bible study, and it incorporates the time-tested stages of Bible reading: observation, interpretation, and application. Prompts are provided on your bookmark to help you observe, interpret, and apply the Scriptures. You will also be prompted to use simple and accessible tools as you study. You will grow in confidence and find your pace as you practice observing, interpreting, and applying the Scriptures again and again. You can use this framework to study any book of the Bible.

For Group Study

If you are doing this study as part of a group, you will want to complete each lesson before you meet. Each lesson is divided into five doable steps rather than five assigned days, to allow flexibility. You can work through one step each day or the whole lesson in one sitting. Find the pace that works best for you. No matter how much of the lesson you are able to complete, please don't skip gathering with your Bible study group. You will benefit from your group, and your group will be encouraged by your presence.

Meet Me in the Bible studies are meant to be flexible. Group studies can opt to meet in small groups for discussion and a time of teaching or simply meet for discussion only.

TIPS FOR GROUPS THAT OPT TO MEET FOR BOTH A TIME OF DISCUSSION AND A TIME OF TEACHING

- If this is your group's first Meet Me in the Bible study, be sure each participant is familiar with how to use the Meet Me in the Bible framework before you meet. You can find my video on how to use the Meet Me in the Bible framework at colleensearcy.com/mmibteaching. In this video, I demonstrate how to cross-reference, quickly check other translations, and more, using simple and free digital tools.

- For the first meeting, teachers will want to cover the Getting Started section before discussion. One of the greatest Bible study tools available is the historical context of the Bible book you are studying. To have the best chance of interpreting the Scriptures correctly, you need to know who the author was, whom he was writing to, the literary style he used, and what was happening in the world when he wrote it. I cover the answers to these questions in my "Getting Started" video, which you will find at colleensearcy.com/mmibteaching.

- After answering those preliminary questions, move to small-group discussion. Spend some time getting to know one another by asking questions like, What brought you to this study? Why are you excited to study this content? What piqued your curiosity from the Getting Started questions?

- For all future meetings, you can gather for discussion before or after the teaching. I suggest that you gather *before* the teaching. You will be amazed at the insights gained as each participant shares what was discovered during personal study. Confidence will grow as you learn from one another's discoveries. Tips for discussion:

  - The prompts on your bookmark make good points of discussion. (What did you learn from the repeated words? What was hard to understand? What did you learn about people?)
  - Content-specific discussion questions for each lesson can be found in Tool 7 of the Tool Kit.
  - Additional historical context is given in the questions in Tool 7 of the Tool Kit.
  - The bounce questions in Tool 7 of the Tool Kit are intended to jumpstart discussion and provide an easy transition to the content.
  - Discussion leaders may use as many or as few discussion questions from Tool 7 as they'd like. These questions were written to help you think deeply about the text. Many of the questions do not have one right answer and are meant to encourage further thought and robust discussion. Questions with one correct answer (e.g., What did Paul say about sin in verse 12?) can feel like a quiz rather than an invitation into conversation.

- Discussion leaders *do* want to plan which questions they will cover and think through their own answers before the group meets. They *do not* need to feel pressure to answer every question that surfaces during Bible study. The purpose of Bible study is not to impress with our knowledge; it is to grow in our knowledge of and love for God as we get to know him better through the study of his word. Enjoy being a colearner with those you are studying alongside. If the questions that surface are not answered in the teaching time, you can circle back with your group after you've had time to think further about them.

- Use the prayer pages in Tool 6 of the Tool Kit to record personal prayer requests and the prayers of those you are studying alongside.

TIPS FOR GROUPS THAT OPT TO MEET FOR DISCUSSION ONLY

- If this is your group's first Meet Me in the Bible study, be sure each participant watches my video on how to use the Meet Me in the Bible framework before you meet. You can find it at colleensearcy.com/mmibteaching. In this video, I demonstrate how to cross-reference, quickly check other translations, and more, using simple and free digital tools.
- For the first meeting, be prepared to discuss the Getting Started section. One of the greatest Bible study tools available is the historical context of the Bible book you are studying. To have the best chance of interpreting the Scriptures correctly, you need to know who the author was, whom he was writing to, the literary style he used, and what was happening in the world when he wrote it. I answer these questions in my "Getting Started" video at colleensearcy.com/mmibteaching.
- Spend some time getting to know one another by asking questions like, What brought you to this study? Why are you excited to study this content? What piqued your curiosity from the Getting Started questions?
- For all future meetings:
  - The prompts on your bookmark make good points of discussion: What did you learn from the repeated words? What was hard to understand? What did you learn about people?
  - Content-specific discussion questions for each lesson can be found in Tool 7 of the Tool Kit.
  - The bounce questions in Tool 7 of the Tool Kit are intended to jumpstart discussion and provide an easy transition to the content.

- Additional historical context is given in the questions found in Tool 7 of the Tool Kit.
- Discussion leaders may use as many or as few discussion questions from Tool 7 as they'd like. These questions were written to help you think deeply about the text. Many of the questions do not have one right answer and are meant to encourage further thought and robust discussion. Questions with one correct answer (e.g., What did Paul say about sin in verse 12?) can feel like a quiz rather than an invitation into conversation.

- Discussion leaders *do* want to plan on which questions they will cover and think through their own answers before the group meets. They *do not* need to feel pressure to answer every question that surfaces during Bible study. The purpose of Bible study is not to impress with our knowledge; it is to grow in our knowledge of and love for God as we get to know him better through the study of his word. When stumped by a question, you can say something like, "That is a great question! I'd like to give that more thought and circle back next time we meet." Then have fun studying! Enjoy being a colearner with those you are studying alongside. Ask God to help you with the questions that surface. He is delighted to meet you in the Bible. What a great discussion you will have the next time you meet!
- Use the prayer pages in Tool 6 of the Tool Kit to record personal prayer requests and the prayers of those you are studying alongside.

For Individual Study

- If you are doing this study on your own, you will want to begin by watching my video on how to use the Meet Me in the Bible framework. You can find it at colleensearcy.com/mmibteaching. In this video, I demonstrate how to cross-reference, quickly check other translations, and more, using simple and free digital tools.

- Be sure to complete the Getting Started section before diving in to study the passages of Scripture. One of the greatest Bible study tools available is the historical context of the Bible book you are studying. When you study a passage that is hard to understand, overlay the passage with the context. To have the best chance of interpreting the Scriptures correctly, we need to know who the author was, whom he was writing to, the literary style he used, and what was happening in the world when he wrote it. I answer these questions in my "Getting Started" video at colleensearcy.com/mmibteaching.
- After completing the Getting Started section, each lesson is divided into five doable steps rather than five assigned days, to allow flexibility. You can work through one step each day or work through the whole lesson in one sitting. Find the pace that works best for you.
- For a deeper dive, use the questions in Tool 7 of the Tool Kit. Additional historical context is also given within the questions. These questions were written to help you think deeply about the text.
- Use the prayer pages in Tool 6 of the Tool Kit to record your prayers while you study.

What's Included in This Study

Bible Study Bookmark

All Meet Me in the Bible studies include a bookmark with the time-tested stages of Bible reading (Observe, Interpret, and Apply) on the front. You will see the five-step framework for reading the Bible on the back of the bookmark, including prompts to help you observe, interpret, and apply the Scriptures. You will also be prompted to pause in your study to listen to and enjoy God. He wants to meet you in your study of the Bible! Although the Bible study bookmark and the Bible study book were designed to work together, your bookmark can also be used alone. It was designed to help you study any book of the Bible, and my hope is that you will use your bookmark again and again.

Bible Study Book

The book includes word-for-word Bible text. Mark it up! If you love highlighters, highlight away! If you prefer to draw symbols, grab colored pencils and go for it. Or simply underline with your favorite pen. Your Bible study book also includes titles and designated spaces that correspond with the titles and prompts on your bookmark. Additionally, you will find blank note pages throughout your book to use as you wish. Draw a chart, sketch an image, or write the lyrics to a song. Each lesson concludes with an important wrap-up question to prompt you to consider what you discovered in the Scriptures.

Meet Me in the Bible Tool Kit

Tool 1: *Bible Timeline.* Place an *X* on the simple timeline of the Bible to indicate where the scriptures you are studying land in the whole story of the Bible.

Tool 2: *Map.* Referencing a map while studying is a helpful reminder that these are stories of real people in real places.

Tool 3: *Bible Genres.* Knowing the literary style of the book of the Bible you are studying is key to correct interpretation. Just as you would approach the poems of Wordsworth differently than you would approach a history book about World War II, there are nuances to different literary styles in the Bible that must be kept in mind while interpreting and applying the Scriptures. Use this resource to identify the literary style of the book you are studying.

Tool 4: *Attributes of God.* You will be prompted to use this tool each week. You may want to mark it with a paper clip so you can turn there easily. The ultimate goal of Bible study is to know and love God, and my prayer is that your hope will be further anchored in him as you are reminded of his attributes.

Tool 5: *Bookmark Content.* All the information on your bookmark is included here for your convenience.

Tool 6: *Prayer Pages.* Use these pages to record personal prayers and prayer requests of those studying alongside you.

Tool 7: *Questions for Further Thought and Discussion.* Use as many or as few of these questions as you'd like in your individual or group study. Additional historical context is included in the questions. The bounce questions are intended to jumpstart discussion and provide an easy transition to the content. The remaining questions were written to help you think deeply about the text.

Additional Tools for Your Study

1. *Different Bible translations.* Reading Scripture verses in different Bible translations can give helpful insight as you study. This book includes the ESV translation. Other translations I recommend are the New International Version (NIV), the New Living Translation (NLT), the Christian Standard Bible (CSB), and the New American Standard Bible (NASB). I use The Message as a commentary when I study.
2. *Dictionary and thesaurus.* Look up unfamiliar words as well as "church" words such as *atonement*, *propitiation*, and *covenant*. You will be surprised how much clarity can be gained by reading simple definitions and synonyms in a dictionary or thesaurus.[1]
3. *Cross-references.* Cross-references are included in study Bibles, usually in the middle or at the bottom of a page. A cross-reference is a marker in the Bible pointing to other passages of Scripture with related words and themes. It is usually designated with a superscript (tiny, raised) letter. Cross-referencing is a way to use Scripture to rightly interpret Scripture. You can also use digital tools to cross-reference.[2]
4. *Study Bible footnotes.* If you have a study Bible, the provided footnotes give helpful insights.[3] Wait to check footnotes until after you've observed the text and attempted interpretation using other translations, a dictionary, and cross-references. Resist the temptation to jump to someone else's thoughts before observing and interpreting on your own. Enjoy being curious and see what you discover!

5. *Commentaries*. Commentaries can be helpful in Bible study, but wait to use commentaries until after you've observed the text and attempted interpretation using other translations, a dictionary, and cross-references. Ask God for insight as you study, and be willing to wait to hear from him. Again, resist the temptation to jump to someone else's thoughts before observing and interpreting on your own. For help choosing commentaries, begin by asking trusted leaders about their favorites.[4]

The ultimate goal of Bible study is to know and love God. So observe, interpret, apply, and enjoy God! Stay in conversation with him, asking him to help you understand the Scriptures. Ask him your hard questions. Listen to him. He wants to meet you in your study of the Bible!

WHY STUDY COLOSSIANS AND PHILEMON?

Colossians and Philemon are epistles, or letters, written by the apostle Paul. Paul wrote these letters while he was under house arrest in Rome. I included these letters in a single study because the Colossian church met in Philemon's house. What was it like to be a Colossian when Paul wrote this letter?

- *Colossae was a melting pot of cultures and belief systems.* It was located near the crossroads of two once-important and well-traveled highways, attributing to the diversity of the population. The Colossian church included converts from all sorts of religious, cultural, and philosophical backgrounds including Greeks, Romans, Jews, and Scythians.

- *There was confusion in the church about how to practice Christianity.* Syncretism, the blending of religious beliefs and traditions, was common in the Colossian church. Certain practices and regulations from different religious backgrounds were being added to the gospel. Although believers in Colossae had placed their faith in the Lord Jesus for salvation, they were in the early stages of learning to follow him and live according to his teachings. The man of the house was given almost limitless power over those in his household according to Roman law. Paul's instructions to every member of the Roman household—acknowledging women, children, and bondservants in the same way he acknowledged men—would have been shocking and full of hope. The story of Philemon and his bondservant Onesimus is especially powerful, demonstrating how the practice of the gospel makes right what is broken in the world.

- *Many Colossians lived in fear.* History informs us that Colossae was hit by a natural disaster—a devastating earthquake—about the same time Paul wrote this letter. They were also afraid of the supernatural. Colossians were plagued with fear of the gods, evil spirits, and life beyond the grave. Many wore magical charms and practiced incantations, some even abusing their bodies in order to appease the gods and ward off evil spirits.

- Paul's words called for unity amid diversity.
- Paul's letter brought clarity where there was confusion.
- The gospel he preached introduced hope in the thick of fear.

There is much to learn from Paul's letters to this early church family. May we be reminded of the unity amid diversity, the clarity, and the hope that the gospel still calls us into. Enjoy getting to know God better and better as he meets you in your study of Colossians and Philemon.

Joyfully,
COLLEEN SEARCY

GETTING STARTED IN COLOSSIANS AND PHILEMON

We have our best chance of understanding Colossians and Philemon if we overlay the text in these epistles with important context. Below are context questions to address before you begin the study.[5]

1. Who wrote these books?

2. When were these books written? Turn to Tool 1 in the Tool Kit. Place an *X* on the timeline to determine where the events recorded in these letters land in the whole story of the Bible.

3. To whom were they written, and for what purpose?

4. In what literary style were these books written? Turn to Tool 3 in the Tool Kit for help identifying the genre.[6]

5. What are the central themes of these books?

1
THE FRUIT OF THE GOSPEL

Colossians 1:1–14

THE FRUIT OF THE GOSPEL

Colossians 1:1–14

1 Paul, an apostle of Christ Jesus by the will of God, and Timothy our brother,

2 To the saints and faithful brothers in Christ at Colossae:

Grace to you and peace from God our Father.

3 We always thank God, the Father of our Lord Jesus Christ, when we pray for you, 4 since we heard of your faith in Christ Jesus and of the love that you have for all the saints, 5 because of the hope laid up for you in heaven. Of this you have heard before in the word of the truth, the gospel, 6 which has come to you, as indeed in the whole world it is bearing fruit and increasing—as it also does among you, since the day you heard it and understood the grace of God in truth, 7 just as you learned it from Epaphras our beloved fellow servant. He is a faithful minister of Christ on your behalf 8 and has made known to us your love in the Spirit.

9 And so, from the day we heard, we have not ceased to pray for you, asking that you may be filled with the knowledge of his will in all spiritual wisdom and understanding, 10 so as to walk in a manner worthy of the Lord, fully pleasing to him: bearing fruit in every good work and increasing in the knowledge of God; 11 being strengthened with all power, according to his glorious might, for all endurance and patience with joy; 12 giving thanks to the Father, who has qualified you to share in the inheritance of the saints in light. 13 He has delivered us from the domain of darkness and transferred us to the kingdom of his beloved Son, 14 in whom we have redemption, the forgiveness of sins.

OBSERVE: WHAT DOES THE PASSAGE SAY?

Step 1: Setting and Summary

Key Characters and Locations

CHARACTERS:

- *Paul.* An apostle of Christ Jesus.
- *Timothy.* Coauthor of the letter.
- *The saints at Colossae.* Who Paul is writing to.
- *Epaphras.* A minister of Christ to the Colossians; he is from Colossae.

LOCATIONS:

- *Colossae.* City in modern-day Turkey close to Laodicea.

See if you can find the location(s) on the map in Tool 2 of the Tool Kit.

Summary of the Passage

What Stood Out to You or Piqued Your Curiosity?

Step 2: Key Words and Phrases

Remember to look at the prompts on your Bible study bookmark as you observe the text.

- *Saints (3 times).* NIV translation: "God's holy people, faithful brothers and sisters in Christ."
- *Knowledge (2 times).* Thinking back to the context, many religious backgrounds were represented in this new church and syncretism was a challenge. It makes sense that Paul prayed for them to increase in their knowledge of God.
- *Bearing fruit (2 times).*

Remember to enjoy God and listen as you study. Move to a time of prayer after you observe, recording your prayer on the prayer pages in Tool 6 of the Tool Kit.

NOTES

INTERPRET: WHAT DOES THE PASSAGE MEAN?

Step 3: What Was Hard to Understand?

Questions

- *What is an apostle, exactly?*
- *Who is Timothy and what is his role?*

Insights from Cross-References, Other Translations, and/or the Context

Remember that historical context is one of the greatest Bible study tools available. Keep asking the questions Who wrote this? When did he write it? Where does this land in the whole story of the Bible? How would these words land on the ears of the original hearers?

- *What is an apostle, exactly?* Dictionary definition: An apostle is one sent on a mission, such as "one of [the] authoritative New Testament group sent out to preach the gospel and made up especially of Christ's 12 original disciples and Paul."[7]
- *Who is Timothy and what is his role?* From cross-references 1 Thessalonians 3:2 and 1 Corinthians 4:17, Timothy is considered a brother and coworker in the gospel, sent out to exhort the saints in the faith. Paul referred to him as his beloved and faithful child in the Lord. Paul is a spiritual father to Timothy. We learn from cross-reference Acts 16:1 that Timothy's mother was a Jewish believer and his father was Greek.

Remember to turn to the Questions for Further Thought and Discussion in Tool 7 for a deeper dive. Additional historical context is also given within the questions in Tool 7.

Step 4: What Did You Learn about God?

Refer to the attributes of God in Tool 4 if needed.

Remember to enjoy God and listen as you study. Move to a time of prayer after you interpret, recording your prayer on the prayer pages in Tool 6.

NOTES

APPLY: HOW WILL YOU APPLY THE PASSAGE?

Step 5: What Did You Learn about People?

Others

Remember to look at the prompts on your Bible study bookmark as you apply the text.

Yourself

- *Is there a command to obey? An example to follow? A sin to confess? A warning to heed? An encouragement to receive?*
- *What action step will you take?*

Wrap Up: What Did You Discover in the Scriptures That Was Important to You?

Remember to enjoy God and listen as you study. Move to a time of prayer after you apply, recording your prayer on the prayer pages in Tool 6.

2
THE HEART OF THE GOSPEL

Colossians 1:15–23

THE HEART OF THE GOSPEL

Colossians 1:15–23

15 He is the image of the invisible God, the firstborn of all creation. 16 For by
him all things were created, in heaven and on earth, visible and invisible,
whether thrones or dominions or rulers or authorities—all things were
created through him and for him. 17 And he is before all things, and in him
all things hold together. 18 And he is the head of the body, the church. He is
the beginning, the firstborn from the dead, that in everything he might be
preeminent. 19 For in him all the fullness of God was pleased to dwell, 20 and
through him to reconcile to himself all things, whether on earth or in heaven,
making peace by the blood of his cross.

21 And you, who once were alienated and hostile in mind, doing evil deeds,
22 he has now reconciled in his body of flesh by his death, in order to present you holy and blameless and above reproach before him, 23 if indeed you
continue in the faith, stable and steadfast, not shifting from the hope of
the gospel that you heard, which has been proclaimed in all creation under
heaven, and of which I, Paul, became a minister.

OBSERVE: WHAT DOES THE PASSAGE SAY?

Step 1: Setting and Summary

Key Characters and Locations

CHARACTERS:

LOCATIONS:

Summary of the Passage

What Stood Out to You or Piqued Your Curiosity?

Step 2: Key Words and Phrases

NOTES

INTERPRET: WHAT DOES THE PASSAGE MEAN?

Step 3: What Was Hard to Understand?

Questions

Insights from Cross-References, Other Translations, and the Context

Step 4: What Did You Learn about God?

Refer to the attributes of God in Tool 4 if needed.

NOTES

APPLY: HOW WILL YOU APPLY THE PASSAGE?

Step 5: What Did You Learn about People?

Others

Yourself

Wrap Up: What Did You Discover in the Scriptures That Was Important to You?

3

THE RICHES OF THE GOSPEL

Colossians 1:24–2:7

THE RICHES OF THE GOSPEL

Colossians 1:24–2:7

24 Now I rejoice in my sufferings for your sake, and in my flesh I am filling up what is lacking in Christ's afflictions for the sake of his body, that is, the church, 25 of which I became a minister according to the stewardship from God that was given to me for you, to make the word of God fully known, 26 the mystery hidden for ages and generations but now revealed to his saints. 27 To them God chose to make known how great among the Gentiles are the riches of the glory of this mystery, which is Christ in you, the hope of glory. 28 Him we proclaim, warning everyone and teaching everyone with all wisdom, that we may present everyone mature in Christ. 29 For this I toil, struggling with all his energy that he powerfully works within me.

2:1 For I want you to know how great a struggle I have for you and for those at Laodicea and for all who have not seen me face to face, 2 that their hearts may be encouraged, being knit together in love, to reach all the riches of full assurance of understanding and the knowledge of God's mystery, which is Christ, 3 in whom are hidden all the treasures of wisdom and knowledge. 4 I say this in order that no one may delude you with plausible arguments. 5 For though I am absent in body, yet I am with you in spirit, rejoicing to see your good order and the firmness of your faith in Christ.

6 Therefore, as you received Christ Jesus the Lord, so walk in him, 7 rooted and built up in him and established in the faith, just as you were taught, abounding in thanksgiving.

OBSERVE: WHAT DOES THE PASSAGE SAY?

Step 1: Setting and Summary

Key Characters and Locations

CHARACTERS:

LOCATIONS:

Summary of the Passage

What Stood Out to You or Piqued Your Curiosity?

Step 2: Key Words and Phrases

NOTES

INTERPRET: WHAT DOES THE PASSAGE MEAN?

Step 3: What Was Hard to Understand?

Questions

Insights from Cross-References, Other Translations, and the Context

Step 4: What Did You Learn about God?

Refer to the attributes of God in Tool 4 if needed.

NOTES

APPLY: HOW WILL YOU APPLY THE PASSAGE?

Step 5: What Did You Learn about People?

Others

Yourself

Wrap Up: What Did You Discover in the Scriptures That Was Important to You?

4
ALIVE IN CHRIST

Colossians 2:8–23

ALIVE IN CHRIST

Colossians 2:8–23

8 See to it that no one takes you captive by philosophy and empty deceit, according to human tradition, according to the elemental spirits of the world, and not according to Christ. 9 For in him the whole fullness of deity dwells bodily, 10 and you have been filled in him, who is the head of all rule and authority. 11 In him also you were circumcised with a circumcision made without hands, by putting off the body of the flesh, by the circumcision of Christ, 12 having been buried with him in baptism, in which you were also raised with him through faith in the powerful working of God, who raised him from the dead. 13 And you, who were dead in your trespasses and the uncircumcision of your flesh, God made alive together with him, having forgiven us all our trespasses, 14 by canceling the record of debt that stood against us with its legal demands. This he set aside, nailing it to the cross. 15 He disarmed the rulers and authorities and put them to open shame, by triumphing over them in him.

16 Therefore let no one pass judgment on you in questions of food and drink, or with regard to a festival or a new moon or a Sabbath. 17 These are a shadow of the things to come, but the substance belongs to Christ. 18 Let no one disqualify you, insisting on asceticism and worship of angels, going on in detail about visions, puffed up without reason by his sensuous mind, 19 and not holding fast to the Head, from whom the whole body, nourished and knit together through its joints and ligaments, grows with a growth that is from God.

20 If with Christ you died to the elemental spirits of the world, why, as if you were still alive in the world, do you submit to regulations— 21 "Do not handle, Do not taste, Do not touch" 22 (referring to things that all perish as they are used)—according to human precepts and teachings? 23 These have indeed an appearance of wisdom in promoting self-made religion and asceticism and severity to the body, but they are of no value in stopping the indulgence of the flesh.

OBSERVE: WHAT DOES THE PASSAGE SAY?

Step 1: Setting and Summary

Key Characters and Locations

CHARACTERS:

LOCATIONS:

Summary of the Passage

What Stood Out to You or Piqued Your Curiosity?

Step 2: Key Words and Phrases

NOTES

INTERPRET: WHAT DOES THE PASSAGE MEAN?

Step 3: What Was Hard to Understand?

Questions

Insights from Cross-References, Other Translations, and the Context

Step 4: What Did You Learn about God?

Refer to the attributes of God in Tool 4 if needed.

NOTES

APPLY: HOW WILL YOU APPLY THE PASSAGE?

Step 5: What Did You Learn about People?

Others

Yourself

Wrap Up: What Did You Discover in the Scriptures That Was Important to You?

5
WHAT TO PUT OFF AND WHAT TO PUT ON

Colossians 3:1–17

WHAT TO PUT OFF AND WHAT TO PUT ON

Colossians 3:1–17

1 If then you have been raised with Christ, seek the things that are above,
where Christ is, seated at the right hand of God. 2 Set your minds on things
that are above, not on things that are on earth. 3 For you have died, and your
life is hidden with Christ in God. 4 When Christ who is your life appears, then
you also will appear with him in glory.

5 Put to death therefore what is earthly in you: sexual immorality, impurity,
passion, evil desire, and covetousness, which is idolatry. 6 On account of these
the wrath of God is coming. 7 In these you too once walked, when you were
living in them. 8 But now you must put them all away: anger, wrath, malice,
slander, and obscene talk from your mouth. 9 Do not lie to one another,
seeing that you have put off the old self with its practices 10 and have put
on the new self, which is being renewed in knowledge after the image of its
creator. 11 Here there is not Greek and Jew, circumcised and uncircumcised,
barbarian, Scythian, slave, free; but Christ is all, and in all.

12 Put on then, as God's chosen ones, holy and beloved, compassionate
hearts, kindness, humility, meekness, and patience, 13 bearing with one another and, if one has a complaint against another, forgiving each other; as
the Lord has forgiven you, so you also must forgive. 14 And above all these
put on love, which binds everything together in perfect harmony. 15 And
let the peace of Christ rule in your hearts, to which indeed you were called
in one body. And be thankful. 16 Let the word of Christ dwell in you richly,
teaching and admonishing one another in all wisdom, singing psalms and
hymns and spiritual songs, with thankfulness in your hearts to God. 17 And
whatever you do, in word or deed, do everything in the name of the Lord
Jesus, giving thanks to God the Father through him.

OBSERVE: WHAT DOES THE PASSAGE SAY?

Step 1: Setting and Summary

Key Characters and Locations

CHARACTERS:

LOCATIONS:

Summary of the Passage

What Stood Out to You or Piqued Your Curiosity?

Step 2: Key Words and Phrases

NOTES

INTERPRET: WHAT DOES THE PASSAGE MEAN?

Step 3: What Was Hard to Understand?

Questions

Insights from Cross-References, Other Translations, and the Context

Step 4: What Did You Learn about God?

Refer to the attributes of God in Tool 4 if needed.

NOTES

APPLY: HOW WILL YOU APPLY THE PASSAGE?

Step 5: What Did You Learn about People?

Others

Yourself

Wrap Up: What Did You Discover in the Scriptures That Was Important to You?

6
WHATEVER YOU DO, PART 1: INSTRUCTIONS TO THE COMMON ROMAN HOUSEHOLD

Colossians 3:18–4:6

WHATEVER YOU DO, PART 1: INSTRUCTIONS TO THE COMMON ROMAN HOUSEHOLD

Colossians 3:18–4:6

18 Wives, submit to your husbands, as is fitting in the Lord. 19 Husbands, love
your wives, and do not be harsh with them. 20 Children, obey your parents in
everything, for this pleases the Lord. 21 Fathers, do not provoke your children,
lest they become discouraged. 22 Bondservants, obey in everything those who
are your earthly masters, not by way of eye-service, as people-pleasers, but
with sincerity of heart, fearing the Lord. 23 Whatever you do, work heartily, as
for the Lord and not for men, 24 knowing that from the Lord you will receive the
inheritance as your reward. You are serving the Lord Christ. 25 For the wrong-
doer will be paid back for the wrong he has done, and there is no partiality.

4:1 Masters, treat your bondservants justly and fairly, knowing that you also
have a Master in heaven.

2 Continue steadfastly in prayer, being watchful in it with thanksgiving.
3 At the same time, pray also for us, that God may open to us a door for the
word, to declare the mystery of Christ, on account of which I am in prison—
4 that I may make it clear, which is how I ought to speak.

5 Walk in wisdom toward outsiders, making the best use of the time. 6 Let
your speech always be gracious, seasoned with salt, so that you may know
how you ought to answer each person.

OBSERVE: WHAT DOES THE PASSAGE SAY?

Step 1: Setting and Summary

Key Characters and Locations

CHARACTERS:

LOCATIONS:

Summary of the Passage

What Stood Out to You or Piqued Your Curiosity?

Step 2: Key Words and Phrases

NOTES

INTERPRET: WHAT DOES THE PASSAGE MEAN?

Step 3: What Was Hard to Understand?

Questions

Insights from Cross-References, Other Translations, and the Context

Step 4: What Did You Learn about God?

Refer to the attributes of God in Tool 4 if needed.

NOTES

APPLY: HOW WILL YOU APPLY THE PASSAGE?

Step 5: What Did You Learn about People?

Others

Yourself

Wrap Up: What Did You Discover in the Scriptures That Was Important to You?

7

WHATEVER YOU DO, PART 2: SERVING THE BODY OF CHRIST

Colossians 4:7–18

WHATEVER YOU DO, PART 2: SERVING THE BODY OF CHRIST

Colossians 4:7–18

7 Tychicus will tell you all about my activities. He is a beloved brother and
faithful minister and fellow servant in the Lord. 8 I have sent him to you for
this very purpose, that you may know how we are and that he may encourage your hearts, 9 and with him Onesimus, our faithful and beloved brother,
who is one of you. They will tell you of everything that has taken place here.

10 Aristarchus my fellow prisoner greets you, and Mark the cousin of Barn-
abas (concerning whom you have received instructions—if he comes to you,
welcome him), 11 and Jesus who is called Justus. These are the only men of
the circumcision among my fellow workers for the kingdom of God, and they
have been a comfort to me. 12 Epaphras, who is one of you, a servant of Christ
Jesus, greets you, always struggling on your behalf in his prayers, that you
may stand mature and fully assured in all the will of God. 13 For I bear him
witness that he has worked hard for you and for those in Laodicea and in
Hierapolis. 14 Luke the beloved physician greets you, as does Demas. 15 Give
my greetings to the brothers at Laodicea, and to Nympha and the church in
her house. 16 And when this letter has been read among you, have it also read
in the church of the Laodiceans; and see that you also read the letter from
Laodicea. 17 And say to Archippus, "See that you fulfill the ministry that you
have received in the Lord."

18 I, Paul, write this greeting with my own hand. Remember my chains.
Grace be with you.

OBSERVE: WHAT DOES THE PASSAGE SAY?

Step 1: Setting and Summary

Key Characters and Locations

CHARACTERS:

LOCATIONS:

Summary of the Passage

What Stood Out to You or Piqued Your Curiosity?

Step 2: Key Words and Phrases

NOTES

INTERPRET: WHAT DOES THE PASSAGE MEAN?

Step 3: What Was Hard to Understand?

Questions

Insights from Cross-References, Other Translations, and the Context

Step 4: What Did You Learn about God?

Refer to the attributes of God in Tool 4 if needed.

NOTES

APPLY: HOW WILL YOU APPLY THE PASSAGE?

Step 5: What Did You Learn about People?

Others

Yourself

Wrap Up: What Did You Discover in the Scriptures That Was Important to You?

8
THE PRACTICE OF THE GOSPEL

Philemon 1–25

THE PRACTICE OF THE GOSPEL

Philemon 1–25

[1] Paul, a prisoner for Christ Jesus, and Timothy our brother,

To Philemon our beloved fellow worker [2] and Apphia our sister and Archippus our fellow soldier, and the church in your house:

[3] Grace to you and peace from God our Father and the Lord Jesus Christ.

[4] I thank my God always when I remember you in my prayers, [5] because I hear of your love and of the faith that you have toward the Lord Jesus and for all the saints, [6] and I pray that the sharing of your faith may become effective for the full knowledge of every good thing that is in us for the sake of Christ. [7] For I have derived much joy and comfort from your love, my brother, because the hearts of the saints have been refreshed through you.

[8] Accordingly, though I am bold enough in Christ to command you to do what is required, [9] yet for love's sake I prefer to appeal to you—I, Paul, an old man and now a prisoner also for Christ Jesus— [10] I appeal to you for my child, Onesimus, whose father I became in my imprisonment. [11] (Formerly he was useless to you, but now he is indeed useful to you and to me.) [12] I am sending him back to you, sending my very heart. [13] I would have been glad to keep him with me, in order that he might serve me on your behalf during my imprisonment for the gospel, [14] but I preferred to do nothing without your consent in order that your goodness might not be by compulsion but of your own accord. [15] For this perhaps is why he was parted from you for a while, that you might have him back forever, [16] no longer as a bondservant but more than a bondservant, as a beloved brother—especially to me, but how much more to you, both in the flesh and in the Lord.

[17] So if you consider me your partner, receive him as you would receive me. [18] If he has wronged you at all, or owes you anything, charge that to my account. [19] I, Paul, write this with my own hand: I will repay it—to say nothing

of your owing me even your own self. [20] Yes, brother, I want some benefit
from you in the Lord. Refresh my heart in Christ.

[21] Confident of your obedience, I write to you, knowing that you will do
even more than I say. [22] At the same time, prepare a guest room for me, for
I am hoping that through your prayers I will be graciously given to you.

[23] Epaphras, my fellow prisoner in Christ Jesus, sends greetings to you,
[24] and so do Mark, Aristarchus, Demas, and Luke, my fellow workers.

[25] The grace of the Lord Jesus Christ be with your spirit.

NOTES

OBSERVE: WHAT DOES THE PASSAGE SAY?

Step 1: Setting and Summary

Key Characters and Locations

CHARACTERS:

LOCATIONS:

Summary of the Passage

What Stood Out to You or Piqued Your Curiosity?

Step 2: Key Words and Phrases

NOTES

INTERPRET: WHAT DOES THE PASSAGE MEAN?

Step 3: What Was Hard to Understand?

Questions

Insights from Cross-References, Other Translations, and the Context

Step 4: What Did You Learn about God?

Refer to the attributes of God in Tool 4 if needed.

NOTES

APPLY: HOW WILL YOU APPLY THE PASSAGE?

Step 5: What Did You Learn about People?

Others

Yourself

Wrap Up: What Did You Discover in the Scriptures That Was Important to You?

MEET ME IN THE BIBLE TOOL KIT

Tool 1

BIBLE TIMELINE

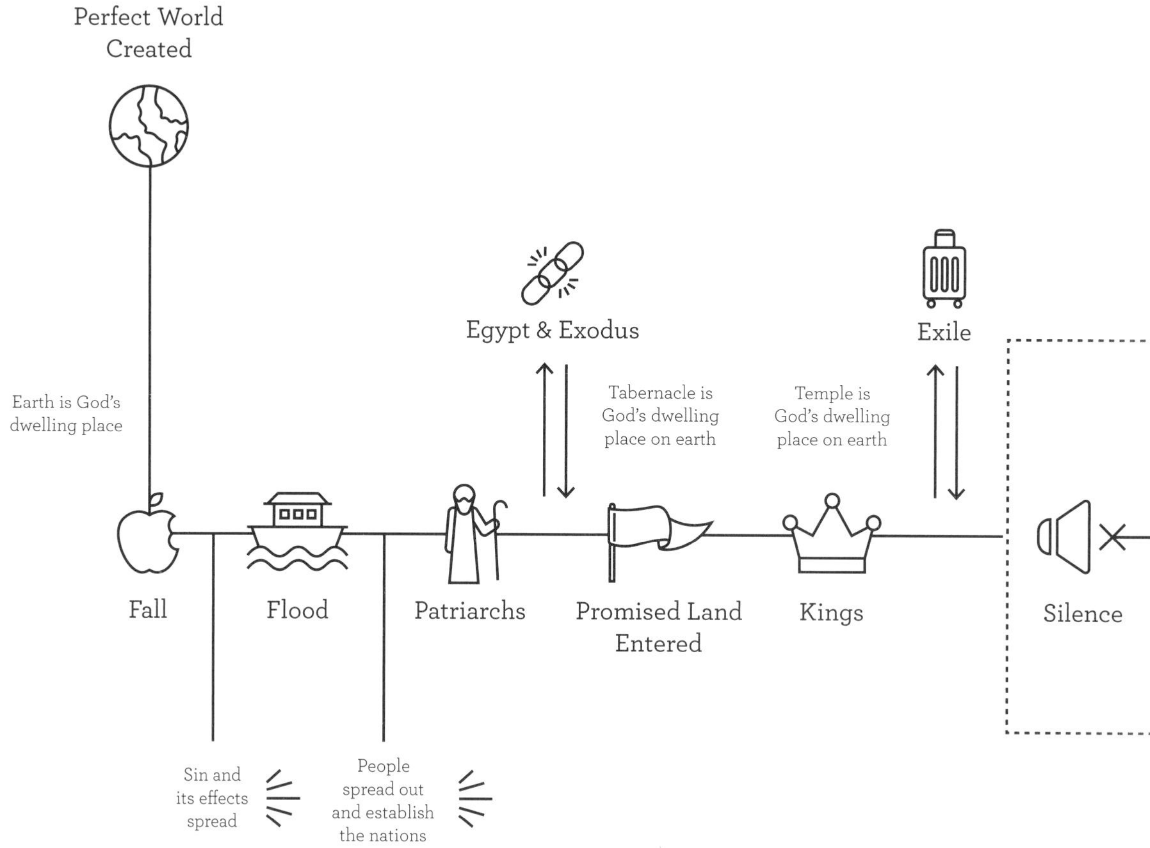

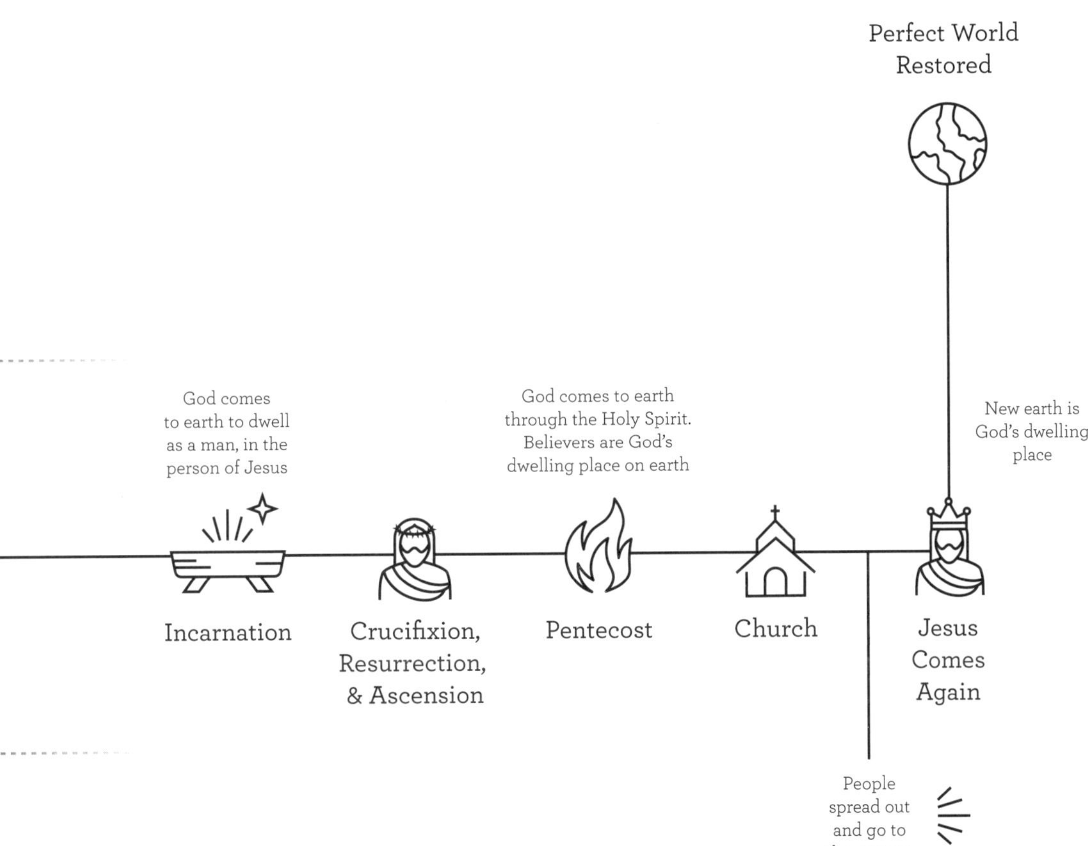
Perfect World
Restored
God comes
to earth to dwell
as a man, in the
person of Jesus
God comes to earth
through the Holy Spirit.
Believers are God's
dwelling place on earth
New earth is
God's dwelling
place
Incarnation
Crucifixion,
Resurrection,
& Ascension
Pentecost
Church
Jesus
Comes
Again
People
spread out
and go to
the nations

Tool 2

MAP: THE SETTING OF COLOSSIANS AND PHILEMON

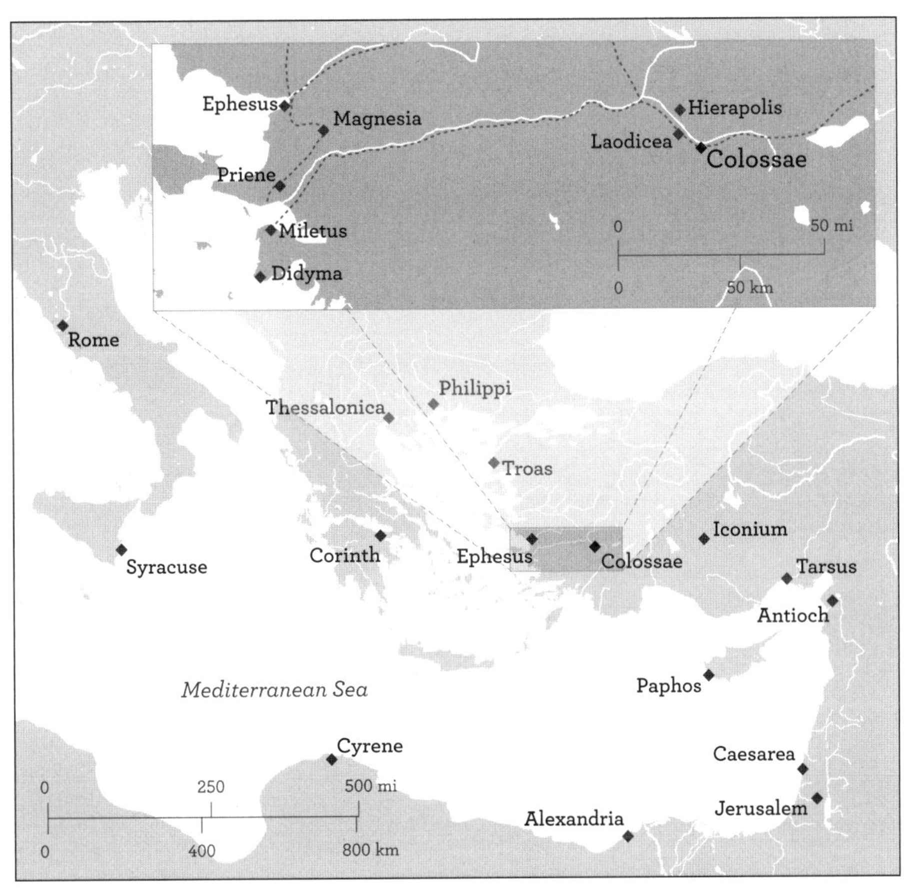

Tool 3

BIBLE GENRES

Knowing the literary style of the book of the Bible you are studying is key to correct interpretation. Just as you would approach the poems of Wordsworth differently than you would approach a history book about World War II, there are nuances to different literary styles in the Bible that must be kept in mind while interpreting and applying the Scriptures. Use this resource to identify the literary style of the book you are studying. Note that several books can be classified in more than one genre.

Genres	Books of the Bible
Apocalyptic. Visionary writings that address future judgment and salvation. Often written using symbolic language.	Daniel, Revelation
Epistle. Letters to Christians in the early church that contain doctrines of the Christian faith and instructions for Christlike living.	Romans, 1–2 Corinthians, Galatians, Ephesians, Philippians, Colossians, 1–2 Thessalonians, 1–2 Timothy, Titus, Philemon, Hebrews, James, 1–2 Peter, 1–3 John, Jude
Gospel. Historical narratives that give testimony to the genealogy, birth, life, death, resurrection, and teachings of Jesus Christ. Each Gospel is written by a different author from a different perspective and with a different emphasis.	Matthew, Mark, Luke, John

Genres	Books of the Bible
Historical Narrative. Narrations of the factual history of Israel and the early church. Historical narratives are recordings of what happened, not necessarily what should have happened had people obeyed God's commands.	Genesis, Exodus, Leviticus, Numbers, Deuteronomy, Joshua, Judges, Ruth, 1–2 Samuel, 1–2 Kings, 1–2 Chronicles, Ezra, Nehemiah, Esther, Jonah, Acts
Poetry. Expressions of joy, thanksgiving, celebration, disappointment, anxiety, and lament in poetic forms.	Psalms, Song of Solomon, Lamentations
Prophecy. God's message to his people spoken through prophets, calling God's people to repentance from sin, warning them of judgment, and revealing events yet to come.	Isaiah, Jeremiah, Ezekiel, Daniel, Hosea, Joel, Amos, Obadiah, Jonah, Micah, Nahum, Habakkuk, Zephaniah, Haggai, Zechariah, Malachi
Wisdom Literature. Writings that address life's basic questions about what it means to live faithful, God-centered lives in both big crises and everyday circumstances.	Job, some Psalms, Proverbs, Ecclesiastes

Tool 4

ATTRIBUTES OF GOD

Attentive. God hears and responds to the needs of his children.

Compassionate. God cares for his children and acts on their behalf.

Creator. God made everything. He is uncreated.

Deliverer. God rescues and saves his children.

Eternal. God is not limited by and exists outside of time.

Faithful. God always keeps his promises.

Generous. God gives what is best and beyond what is deserved.

Glorious. God displays his greatness and worth.

Good. God is what is best and gives what is best.

Holy. God is perfect, pure, and without sin.

Immutable/Unchanging. God never changes. He is the same yesterday, today, and tomorrow.

Incomprehensible. God is beyond our understanding. We can comprehend him in part but not in whole.

Infinite. God has no limits in his person or on his power.

Jealous. God will not share his glory with another. All glory rightfully belongs to him.

Just. God is fair in all his actions and judgments. He cannot overpunish or underpunish.

Loving. God feels and displays infinite, unconditional affection toward his children. His love for them does not depend on their worth, their response, or their merit.

Merciful. God does not give his children the punishment they deserve.

Omnipotent/Almighty. God holds all power. Nothing is too hard for God. What he wills he can accomplish.

Omnipresent. God is fully present everywhere.

Omniscient. God knows everything past, present, and future, all potential and real outcomes, all things micro and macro.

Patient/Long-Suffering. God is untiring and bears with his children.

Provider. God meets the needs of his children.

Refuge. God is a place of safety and protection for his children.

Righteous. God is always good and right.

Self-Existent. God depends on nothing and no one to give him life or existence.

Sovereign. God does everything according to his plan and pleasure. He controls all things.

Transcendant. God is not like humans. He is infinitely higher in being and action.

Truthful. Whatever God speaks or does is truth and reality.

Wise. God knows what is best and acts accordingly. He cannot choose wrongly.

Worthy. God deserves all glory and honor and praise.

Wrathful. God hates all unrighteousness.

Tool 5

BOOKMARK CONTENT

Begin by asking God to reveal himself as you read the Scriptures. Enjoy him and have fun learning and discovering!

Observe: What Does the Passage Say?

Step 1. Setting and Summary

- Read the passage, noting key characters and locations.
- Write a brief summary of the passage (about three to five sentences).
- Record what stood out to you or piqued your curiosity.

Step 2. Key Words and Phrases

- Read the passage, marking the words/phrases that are repeated or emphasized.
- Why do you think the author repeats these words? Look back at the context to help you with your answer (e.g., Who wrote it and to whom was it written?). Write down your insights.
- Are there words for which you need a better understanding (e.g., *propitiation, atonement*)? Use a dictionary or thesaurus to gain insight and note what you discover.
- Read the verses with key words/phrases in two other Bible translations. Jot down what you learn.
- Enjoy God. Talk to him and listen.

Interpret: What Does the Passage Mean?

Step 3. What Was Hard to Understand?

- Read the passage, writing down the questions that surface for you.

- Record insights you gain from the following:
    - Looking up cross-references for verses that are hard to understand.
    - Reading the passage in two other Bible translations.
    - Looking back at the context (e.g., Who wrote it and to whom was it written and when?).

Step 4. What Did You Learn about God?

- What attribute of God stood out to you in this passage?
- How does this attribute of God encourage you to anchor your hope in him? Record your discoveries.
- Enjoy God. Talk to him and listen.

Apply: How Will You Apply the Passage?

Step 5. What Did You Learn about People?

OTHERS

- What did you learn about people in this passage? How does this passage promote a love for others? Write down your thoughts.
- What did you learn that you can share with others (a friend, coworker, family member)? Pray for meaningful conversations this week.

YOURSELF

- Is there a command to obey? An example to follow? A sin to confess? A warning to heed? An encouragement to receive? Record your insights.
- What action step will you take? How will next week be different because you chose to apply what you discovered?
- Enjoy God. Talk to him and listen.

Tool 6

PRAYER PAGES

PRAYER PAGE

PRAYER PAGE

PRAYER PAGE

PRAYER PAGE

PRAYER PAGE

PRAYER PAGE

PRAYER PAGE

Tool 7

QUESTIONS FOR FURTHER THOUGHT AND DISCUSSION

These questions were written to help you think deeply about the text. Additional historical context is also given. Many questions do not have one right answer and are meant to encourage further thought and robust discussion. The bounce questions are intended to jumpstart discussion and provide an easy transition to the content.

Discussion leaders may use as many or as few questions as they'd like. The prompts on your bookmark also make good points of discussion.

Getting Started in Colossians and Philemon

1. Why do you want to study Colossians and Philemon?
2. As you answered the context questions found in "Getting Started in Colossians and Philemon," what new insight did you gain?
3. What piqued your curiosity?
4. Complete the sentence: At the end of this study, I hope to _______________.

The Fruit of the Gospel (Colossians 1:1–14)

- Bounce question: Think of someone you know whose life radically changed for the better. What motivated the change? How did the change impact people closest to her/him?

1. Paul used familial language in his greeting: *brothers* (and *sisters*, NIV) in Christ and God *our Father*. Thinking back to the context, how might familial language be especially helpful for the original hearers? Why do you think Paul would highlight a love for *all* the saints?

2. Epaphras likely became a believer under Paul's ministry and is believed to be the one who planted the church in Colossae. Look up Colossians 4:12–13 and Philemon 23 for more insight about Epaphras. Where is he from (Col. 4:12)? Where was he when Paul wrote this epistle (Philem. 23)? In what way(s) is Epaphras modeling the Lord Jesus?
3. Look over Paul's prayer in Colossians 1:9–12. This provides a wonderful pattern for prayer!
4. Why do you think Paul emphasized the fullness of God's power by using the synonyms "strengthened," "power," and "might"? Think back to what it was like to be a Colossian in AD 62 to help you with your answer.
5. At this moment, which phrase in the prayer would you especially want a friend to pray for you? Why? Whom will you pray these verses for this week?
6. Paul wrote in Colossians 1:12 that believers are qualified to share in the inheritance of the saints. What comes to mind when you hear the word *qualified*? Look up the word *qualified* in a dictionary. What feelings surface when you think about being qualified in Christ?
7. Paul's language in Colossians 1:13, "delivered us" and "transferred us," would have reminded believing Jews of the exodus. How does this add to your understanding of this verse?

The Heart of the Gospel (Colossians 1:15–23)

- Bounce question: What do you expect from someone deemed the "head" of an organization?

1. Sometimes people attach particular attributes to God the Father and other attributes to God the Son. Why do you think this is? How do Colossians 1:15 and Hebrews 1:3 help shape your thinking of God the Father?
2. What do you think Paul meant when he wrote that Jesus was firstborn of all creation and firstborn from the dead? Hint: What did *firstborn* mean to the original hearers?

3. When Paul wrote about rulers and authorities in his letters, he was referring to the unseen spiritual realm (see, e.g., 1 Cor. 15:24; Eph. 1:20–21). Keeping this in mind, make a list of what and who Christ created. How does this list further your understanding of Christ being the firstborn of all creation?

4. What do you think Paul meant when he wrote, ". . . if indeed you continue in the faith" (Col. 1:23)? Do you think he meant that one could lose his/her salvation? Why or why not? Look up this verse in an alternate translation for more insight.

5. History informs us that Colossae was hit by a devastating earthquake around the time Paul wrote this letter. This context adds meaning to Paul's architectural language in verse 23, ". . . if indeed you continue in the faith, stable and steadfast, not shifting from the hope of the gospel." Paul encouraged a city whose foundations were literally shaken not to shift but to remain stable in the faith. What challenge will you apply his words to this week?

The Riches of the Gospel (Colossians 1:24–2:7)

- Bounce question: Do you have a favorite book or movie in which a mystery is solved? Do you enjoy the tension of a good mystery? Why or why not?

1. Colossians 1:24 can be hard to understand. Read 2 Corinthians 1:3–7, then read Colossians 1:24 in an alternate translation. We know nothing was lacking in Christ's suffering. His sacrifice was sufficient. So what was lacking? What do you think Paul meant in Colossians 1:24?

2. Paul often wrote of the mystery, hidden for ages, that had been revealed (Rom. 16:25–26; Eph. 3:8–10). Neither humans nor heavenly beings could have guessed that both Jews and Gentiles would one day have direct and equal access to God through faith in Jesus Christ. What do you think was most surprising for Jewish believers? What do you think was most surprising for Gentile believers?

3. Paul described himself as "struggling with all his energy" for the Colossian and Laodicean believers (Col. 1:29). Is there someone in your life who has struggled on your behalf, deeply desiring your good? How will you emulate this person?

4. Look up the word *plausible* in a dictionary. Name a few of our culture's plausible arguments that could trip up believers today.

5. Paul uses three very different images in Colossians 2:6–7. Why do you think he chose these three metaphors?

Alive in Christ (Colossians 2:8–23)

- Bounce question: How do you determine what is true and not true?

1. What are a few practical steps believers can put into place to "see to it" that they are not taken captive by false teaching (Col. 2:8)?

2. Paul referred to circumcision in Colossians 2:11. Circumcision was the mark of the people of God for thousands of years; literally and symbolically a cutting away of the flesh and shedding of blood. What do you think Paul meant by what he wrote in Colossians 2:11?

3. What do you think the new mark of the people of God is? Look back at Colossians 1:10, and read Galatians 5:6 and Ephesians 2:10 for more insight.

4. The phrases "in Christ" and "with Christ" are found throughout Paul's letters. Union with Christ is an important doctrine of Christianity. To be "in Christ" means that through God's grace, believers participate spiritually in the pivotal moments of Christ's story—his death, his burial, his resurrection, and his ascension. How does this deepen the meaning of baptism (Col. 2:12–13)?

5. Name a few examples of syncretism, the blending of religious beliefs and traditions, found in Colossians 2:16–23. What restrictions or practices are you tempted to add as a qualification for salvation?

What to Put Off and What to Put On (Colossians 3:1–17)

- Bounce question: When you played dress-up as a child, what was your favorite thing to put on?

1. What are some practical ways to seek things that are above rather than things on earth? What do you think Paul meant?
2. What do you think it looks like to put sin to death in everyday life? What steps can be taken, for example, to put covetousness to death?
3. Did Paul think sexual sin was worse than anger? Why or why not?
4. Look up the words *wrath* and *malice* in a dictionary. What is the difference? Now look up the word *slander*. Considering that the Colossian church included people of different religious backgrounds, races, cultures, and socioeconomic status, how might wrath and slander be especially damaging to this new church?
5. In verses 10 and 11, Paul says that as a result of "being renewed after the image of its creator," old divisions of race, religion, and culture must be torn down. In what way(s) is the Colossian church similar to yours? In what way(s) is your church distinct from the Colossian church? What steps can you take to help tear down man-made barriers that do not belong in the kingdom of God?

Whatever You Do, Part 1: Instructions to the Common Roman Household (Colossians 3:18–4:6)

- Bounce question: When you hear the word *submit*, what feelings surface? Why do you think this is?

1. In Colossians 3:18–4:1, Paul addressed those in a typical Roman household. A parallel passage to Colossians 3:18–4:1, Ephesians 5:21–6:4, begins with this command: "[Submit] to one another out of reverence for Christ." How do Colossians 3:17 and Ephesians 5:21 rightly set up the instructions that follow? How do you think this counsel instructs single men and women?

2. It is important to remember the context. When this letter was written, the man of the house had almost limitless power according to Roman law. With this in mind, what do you think was surprising to the original hearers of the letter? Who did Paul assume was attending church and listening to the reading of his letter?

3. Look at Ephesians 5:22–24. Paul instructed wives to submit to their husbands, as is fitting in the Lord. Do Paul's words imply that women should submit to men in general? How is submission a particular way for wives to image the Lord Jesus? Can you think of acts of submission that would not be fitting in the Lord?

4. In what particular ways did Paul call husbands and fathers to image the Lord Jesus?

5. It is important to remember that Paul addressed the world as it was. Paul was not condoning the social structure of the Roman Empire, but instructing how to live within it as a Christian. How do you think Paul's instructions to bondservants and masters apply to you?

6. Paul was under house arrest in Rome when he wrote this letter. Notice his prayer requests. How will his prayer requests form yours in the coming days?

Whatever You Do, Part 2: Serving the Body of Christ (Colossians 4:7–18)

- Bounce question: In what visible ways have you served your church? Invisible ways? Which was more fruitful?

1. Tychicus and Onesimus (Philemon's runaway bondservant) served as the letter carriers from Paul in Rome to Philemon and the church who met in his house in Colossae. How is their seemingly small role still impacting churches today?

2. Look up Acts 19:29 and 27:2, 41–44 to learn more about Aristarchus. Aristarchus had stayed with Paul through a riot and a shipwreck, and he stayed so close to Paul in Rome that Paul called him "my fellow

prisoner" (Col. 4:10). Can you think of someone who has stayed with you no matter no what, offering the ministry of presence?

3. Read Colossians 4:13–16, then look at the map in Tool 2. How might the relationship between the churches in Colossae, Laodicea, and Hierapolis be an example to churches today?

4. What did Aristarchus, Mark, Justus, and Paul have in common (Col. 4:11)? Epaphras and Luke, who are also mentioned in this chapter, were Gentiles. Who was the host of the Laodicean church (4:15)? Onesimus was a slave, and Philemon was his master. Look back at Galatians 3:28 and Colossians 3:11. In what way(s) do the believers listed in Colossians 4:7–17 demonstrate Galatians 3:28 and Colossians 3:11?

5. Look back at Colossians 4:17. What can you learn from Paul's words to Archippus?

The Practice of the Gospel (Philemon 1–25)

- Bounce Question: Describe a time when you experienced reconciliation in a broken relationship.

1. Onesimus was Philemon's runaway bondservant. Because of Philemon 18–19, many assume that Onesimus also stole money from his master. We do not see evidence in Paul's appeal that Philemon was harsh with Onesimus. Onesimus spent time in Rome and somehow came under the influence of Paul, so much so that Paul called him his son. Look back at Colossians 4:9. What did Paul send Onesimus to do, along with Tychicus? How do you think Onesimus felt about carrying this letter to his master? Look back at Colossians 3:22–25 for insight.

2. Review Philemon 8–10. Paul chose not to use his authority to command Philemon to receive Onesimus, but rather he made a gospel appeal, painting a picture of reconciliation. Is there someone you need to appeal to in a similar way?

3. In what way(s) does Paul image the Lord Jesus in this situation (Philem. 17–19)?
4. In what ways does the account of Philemon, Onesimus, and Paul fulfill the instructions given in Colossians 3:1–17? In what ways does the account of Philemon, Onesimus, and Paul bear the fruit of the gospel?
5. What have you learned through the study of Colossians and Philemon that you never want to forget?

NOTES

1. My favorite tool is *Merriam-Webster's Collegiate Dictionary*, 11th ed. (Springfield, MA: Merriam-Webster, 2003), continually updated at https://www.merriam-webster.com.
2. I demonstrate how to use Bible Gateway (https://www.biblegateway.com/) to cross-reference in my introductory video: https://www.colleensearcy.com/.
3. Bible Gateway (https://www.biblegateway.com/) also includes footnotes.
4. I've found Tim Challies's article helpful: "Best Commentaries on Each Book of the Bible" Challies website, accessed April 29, 2024, https://challies.com/.
5. Questions 1–4 are informed by Jen Wilkin, *Women of the Word: How to Study the Bible with Both Our Hearts and Our Minds* (Wheaton, IL: Crossway, 2014).
6. For further study on Bible genres, a helpful resource is Gordon D. Fee and Douglas Stuart, *How to Read the Bible for All Its Worth* (Grand Rapids, MI: Zondervan, 2014).
7. *Merriam-Webster*, s.v. "apostle," accessed April 29, 2024, https://www.merriam-webster.com/.